25 IMPOSSIBLE OBJECTS

That's impossible.

This book is full of things that puzzle scientists, amaze magicians, and baffle just about everybody. Here at Klutz Labs, we had a blast gathering all this weirdness and boxing it up for you. But don't blame us if you look at this stuff and say, "That's impossible." Blame your brain.

Your brain has a lot to do when it's making sense of the world, so sometimes it takes shortcuts. If a shortcut leads in the wrong direction (as shortcuts often do), you can find yourself staring at something that seems totally impossible. You see it, it's right there in front of you, and yet it simply can. not. be.

The stuff in this book will mess with your mind — in a good way. It will stretch how you see the world and how you understand what you see. It may even expand the limits of what you think you can do.

Go ahead — do the impossible.

WEiRD Wobblestone

Tap here.

What do I need?
- The wobblestone
- A smooth, hard, level surface

What do I do?

1 Place the wobblestone on the flat surface with the curved side down.

2 Tap on one end to make it start rocking. It will rock a few times and then start spinning counterclockwise.

3 When it stops, give it a push to make it spin clockwise. It will spin a few times, stop and rock, and then spin in the opposite direction.

What's going on?

Take a look at the curved bottom of the wobblestone. At first glance, it looks perfectly even — like the bottom of a canoe. But if you study it carefully, you'll see that the two ends aren't exactly the same — and neither are the two sides. The differences aren't much, but a little difference is all it takes to make the wobblestone weird.

When you start the wobblestone spinning clockwise, some parts of the curved bottom rub against the table more than others. This uneven rubbing starts the stone rocking. Each time the

stone rocks, its lopsided curve gives it a little push in the counterclockwise direction. Pretty soon, all those pushes add up to make the wobblestone spin counterclockwise.

The weird wobblestone (also known as a rattleback or a rebellious celt) has been around for a long time. Thousands of years ago, people shaped stones to make tools — and some of those tools still rock and spin like this piece of plastic does today. No one knows whether people made wobblestones on purpose — or made tools that just turned out to be wobblestones.

The bottom of a canoe (on the left) is the same on both sides of the center line. The bottom of the wobblestone (on the right) is warped.

MIRROR MONSTER MULTIPLIER

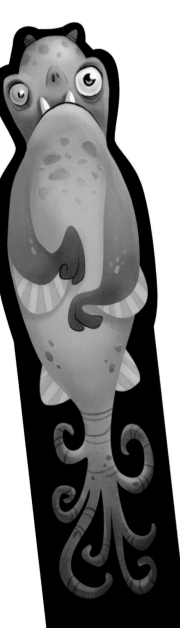

What is it?

A tool for making many monsters

What do I need?

- The hinged mirrors
- The monster stick

What do I do?

1. Peel the clear plastic off each mirror.

2. Fold the mirrors at the hinge, with the shiny sides facing in. Hold the monster stick between the mirrors. How many monsters can you see?

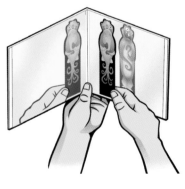

3. Hold the mirrors and the monster stick as shown. Bring the mirrors closer together to reflect a mob of monsters. Our best monster maker counted 28 monsters in the mirrors. Can you beat that?

In the late 1800s, photographers figured out how to use two mirrors to make ▶ reflections of reflections — turning one dog into a pack of identical dogs.

MONSTER CHALLENGES

Can you turn the one-eyed cyclops into a sad two-eyed monster? How about a happy two-eyed monster?

Can you make a circle of sea monsters?

Need a hint? See page 48.

What's going on?

When you hold the monster between two mirrors, you see the reflection of the monster. You also see the reflection of that reflection. Depending on how you hold the monster and the mirrors, you may see a reflection of a reflection of a reflection of a... you get the idea.

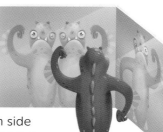

When you're counting sea monsters, pay attention to which side the orange eye is on. The monster on the stick has an orange eye on its right. A reflection swaps right and left, giving the monster an orange eye on its left. But some of the mirror monsters have the orange eye on their right. That's because right and left swap again in the reflection of a reflection.

MONSTER-EYES YOURSELF

What is it?
A chance to change your look (not necessarily in a good way)

What do I need?
- The hinged mirrors
- A table

What do I do?

1. Lay the mirrors side by side on the table. Start with both mirrors lying flat. Lean over and admire yourself. You look gorgeous. So far.

Hold the mirrors by the edges so you don't leave fingerprints.

2. Fold the mirrors at the hinge while studying your face. Can you make your mirror image into every monster on the Monstrous Checklist? You'll need to lift the mirrors off the table to make some of them.

3. Can you make a monster that's not on our list?

If you have trouble making a monster, check out the hint below the picture. To keep them super-secret, we've written the hints in mirror writing.

SUPER FLIP

What is it?
A way to flip upside down (while your feet stay on the ground)

What do I need?
- The hinged mirrors
- A table

What do I do?

1. Stand the edges of the mirrors on the purple lines to the left. In the reflection, the red line will make a red square. (If it doesn't, move the mirrors until it does.) Your mirrors are now at a right angle to each other.

YOU'LL FLIP

MONSTROUS CHECKLIST

Tip: If you have trouble seeing the monster in the mirror, close one eye.

THREE-EYED MONSTER
Hint: Start with the mirrors side by side. Fold them slightly toward each other.

ONE-EYED MONSTER
Hint: Start with the mirrors side by side. Fold them slightly away from each other.

HEADLESS MONSTER
Hint: Start with the mirrors side by side. Fold them away from each other.

FOUR-EYED MONSTER
Hint: Hold the mirrors so one is above the other. Fold them slightly toward each other.

NO-EYED MONSTER
Hint: Hold the mirrors so one is above the other. Fold them slightly away from each other.

UPSIDE-DOWN FOUR-EYED MONSTER
Hint: Try super flip at the bottom of the page.

2. Crouch down until you can see your face in the mirrors. Move to one side so your face is reflected in only one mirror. Wink your eye — and notice which eye your reflection winks. Now move so you see your face in the corner where the mirrors meet. Wink just as you did before, with the same eye. Which eye does your reflection wink? Doesn't that seem a little strange?

3. Pick up the mirrors while admiring your gorgeous face. Hold them at a right angle (or close to it). Now turn them so one mirror is above the other. Trust us — you'll flip.

What's going on?

When you wink your right eye at your reflection in a flat mirror, your mirror self winks its left eye. (The eye that winks is on *your* right, but from the point of view of *your mirror self* it's on the left.) This is the mirror image you are used to seeing, where right and left are reversed.

When you wink your right eye at your reflection in the corner, your mirror self winks its right eye. When two mirrors are at a right angle, each mirror reflects what's in the other mirror. The corner where the mirrors meet shows you the reflection of a reflection of your face or, to put it another way, the reverse of a reverse. This is the face that everyone else sees when they look at you.

When you turn the mirrors so one is above the other, the reflected reflection flips you upside down. And when you change the angle between the mirrors, you create reflections that remove or multiply bits of your face — just the thing for making yourself monstrous.

Mirrors are always tricky. Mirrors reflecting reflections are even trickier.

secret Pictures

What is it?
A hunt for hidden objects

What do I need?
The hinged mirrors

What do I do?
Use your mirrors to transform the teapot and microscope into these secret pictures.

bug-eyed goldfish

5-armed starfish

red-and-white butterfly

fancy daisy

This is no ordinary teapot.

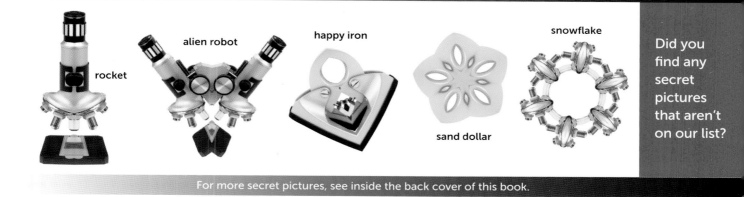

rocket

alien robot

happy iron

sand dollar

snowflake

Did you find any secret pictures that aren't on our list?

For more secret pictures, see inside the back cover of this book.

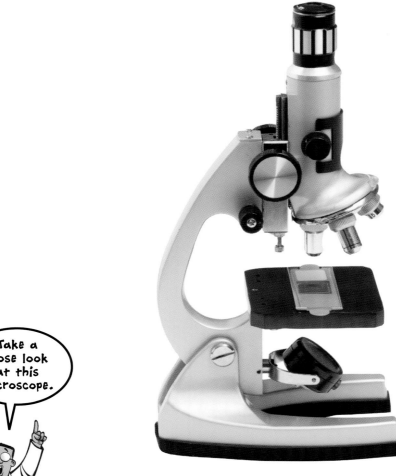

Take a close look at this microscope.

CRAZY SIGN

What is it?
A mysterious road sign guaranteed to baffle your friends

What do I need?
The Crazy Sign

What do I do?

1 Take a look at the sign — an ordinary piece of cardboard with an arrow on each side.

SIDE 1

2 Turn the sign until the arrow is pointing to the right at an upward angle. Grab hold of the two points marked with |. Imagine there's a bar connecting these two points. Flip the sign over the bar so you're looking at the other side.

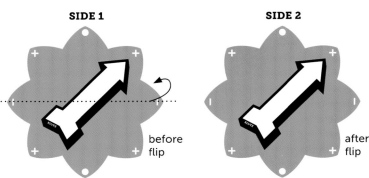

SIDE 1

before flip

SIDE 2

after flip

The arrow is still pointing in the same direction. So you'd think it points the same way on both sides of the card. Right?

3 Now rotate the sign so the arrow points straight up. Grab the points on opposite sides of the sign that are marked with ✖.

Flip the sign over the imaginary bar connecting the ✖s.

SIDE 1

SIDE 2

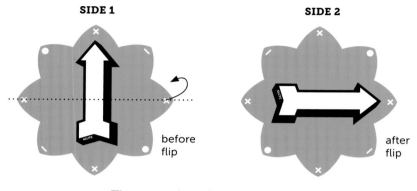

before flip

after flip

The arrow has changed direction — now it points to the side.

4 You're not done yet. Rotate the sign so the arrow points to the left at an upward angle. Grab the points marked with ●. Flip the sign over the imaginary bar connecting the ●s.

SIDE 1

SIDE 2

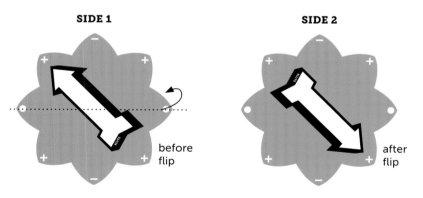

before flip

after flip

The arrow now points in the opposite direction.
WEIRD.

Use the Crazy Sign to spread confusion wherever you go. Practice these moves in front of a mirror before trying them on a friend.

1 Hold the sign by the points marked with | so your friend sees:

Say: **"I'm going to test your sense of direction. Point in the direction the arrow's pointing."**

Now flip the sign over.

On the other side, the arrow points the same way.

2 Now it's going to get interesting. Turn the sign so you are holding the points marked with ✖ and your victim sees:

Say: **"Which way will the arrow be pointing on the other side?"**

Flip the sign over.

When you flip the sign, the arrow points in a new direction.

3 Turn the sign so you are holding the points marked with ● and your victim sees:

Say: **"Let's try another angle. Which way will the arrow on the other side point?"**

Flip the sign again.

When you flip the sign, watch his head explode.

4 Smile and ask:

Want to try that again?

WHAT'S GOING ON?

The way you turn something over changes what you see on the other side.

Take a look at the bird in the corner of page 12. The sign he's carrying points left, toward the edge of the page.

page 12

Turn to page 11. You'll see the same bird from the other side. The sign still points to the edge of the page, but now it's pointing to the right.

Some might say that the signs point in opposite directions. Others will insist they are pointing in the same direction. Depending on how you look at it, they are both right.

page 11

Now we'll show you how to make the arrow on page 11 change direction. (Drumroll, please...)

Fold the corner of page 12 on the dotted line, like this.

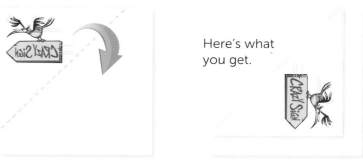

Here's what you get.

You probably aren't surprised. When you folded the corner at a diagonal, you knew you would be changing the direction of the bird.

The Crazy Sign confuses people because they don't see that you are turning it over in different ways.

If people ask you what's going on with the Crazy Sign, we suggest you shrug and say: "It has to do with vector components under rotational transformation." That's how a mathematician would describe what's going on with the arrow — and it sure sounds impressive.

MOE'S ENDLESS TWIST

What is it?

A twisted piece of paper called a Möbius strip.
It has only one side.

What do I need?

Paper that's at least 11 inches (28 cm) long
Tape • A pencil • Scissors • A paper clip

How do I make it?

1 Cut two strips of paper, each about 1-1/2 inches (4 cm) wide and at least 11 inches (28 cm) long.

2 Make one strip into a loop by bringing the ends together. Then turn one end of the strip over so you have a loop with a half-twist. Tape the ends together.

 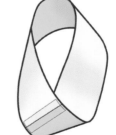

3 You now have a Möbius strip. Repeat step 2 with the other strip.

MOE'S ENDLESS TWIST

What do I do with it?

1 Draw a line down the middle of one Möbius strip. Keep going until you get back to where you started.

2 Take a careful look at your line. Even though you never picked up the pencil to change sides, the line goes all around the inside *and* the outside of the loop. That's because the inside and the outside are the same side.

3 Write **B** and **A** near the edges of the strip. Put a paper clip beside **B** to mark the edge.

4 Start at **A**. Pinch the edge of the strip between your thumb and finger and run your hand along the edge. Eventually, you'll reach the paper clip at **B**. Without taking your fingers off the strip, keep on going. You'll end up back at the **A**, having gone all the way around the loop twice. Your Möbius strip has only one edge.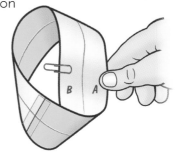

5 What do you think you'll get if you cut your Möbius strip in half along the line you drew? Take off the paper clip and try it.

First, pinch the strip and make a snip with your scissors.

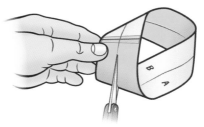

Then, poke one blade of the scissors through the slit you made, and cut along your line.

Twisted Thinking

When you cut your Möbius strip in the middle, you got a big loop with a full twist in it. Cut near one side and you get a big loop linked to a Möbius strip. Totally different results, just from making your cuts in different places. Weird.

August Ferdinand Möbius discovered how to make the Möbius strip back in 1858. Ever since then, people have been marveling at how strange it is and thinking about where its weirdness leads.

For instance, think about what happens if you take a hole punch and make a hole through the Möbius strip. You might think the hole goes from one side of the strip to the other — but you know that the strip only has one side. So where does the hole go from and to?

If you were a two-dimensional person living on the Möbius strip, the hole would give you a surprising shortcut from one location on the one-sided strip to another location on the one-sided strip. That shortcut goes through the third dimension, something that a two-dimensional being living on the strip might have a tough time imagining.

We live in a three-dimensional world. Could there be a way to take a shortcut through the fourth dimension that we haven't figured out yet?

 Did you get what you expected? Do you still have a Möbius strip?

To find out, repeat step 1 to see if the strip has only one side.

 Now find the other Möbius strip you made. This time, rather than cutting the strip in half, start your cut near the edge, as if you were going to cut a skinny ring off the wide ring. (Of course, you've realized by now that there's no way you're going to do anything that simple.) What do you think you'll get?

Start your cut near the edge.

This is one weird piece of paper!

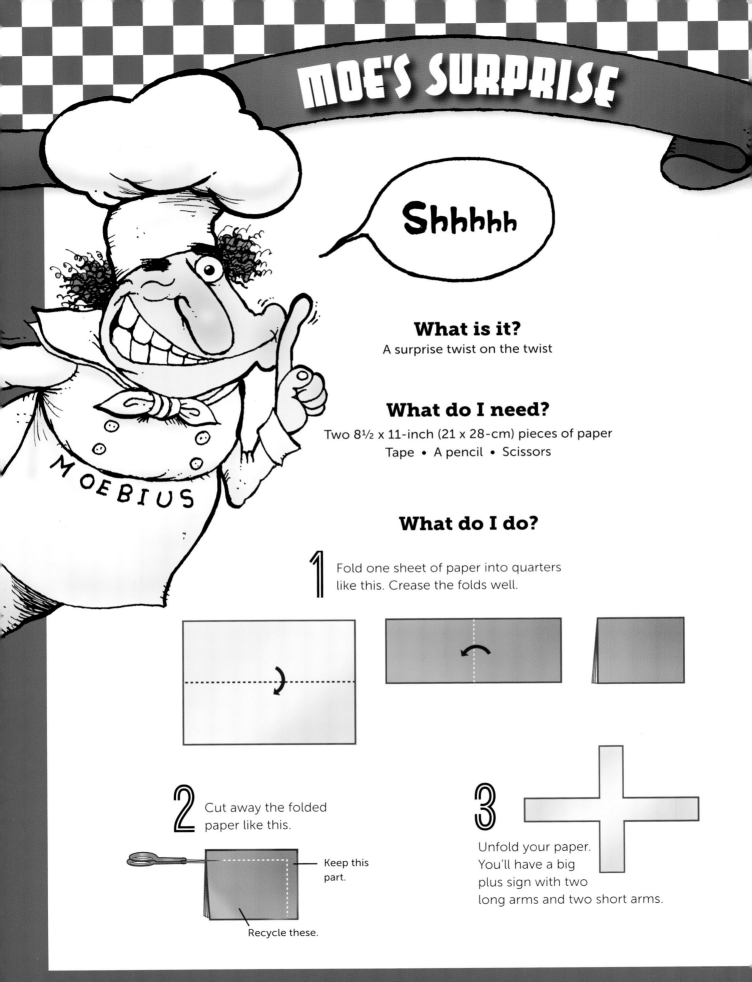

MOE'S SURPRISE

Shhhhh

What is it?

A surprise twist on the twist

What do I need?

Two 8½ x 11-inch (21 x 28-cm) pieces of paper
Tape • A pencil • Scissors

What do I do?

1 Fold one sheet of paper into quarters like this. Crease the folds well.

2 Cut away the folded paper like this.

Keep this part.

Recycle these.

3 Unfold your paper. You'll have a big plus sign with two long arms and two short arms.

4 Pull the long arms toward you and tape the ends together to make a loop.

5 Bring the ends of the short arms together like this. Tape them.

6 What do you think will happen if you cut on the crease down the middle of the smaller loop? Make your best guess, then try the experiment.

Cut here.

7 What do you think will happen if you cut on the remaining crease? Try it. Were you surprised?

8 Now go for something really strange. Find your other sheet of paper. Repeat steps 1–5, but this time put in a half twist each time you connect the arms. That will make each loop a Möbius strip. What will happen when you cut them as you did in steps 6 and 7?

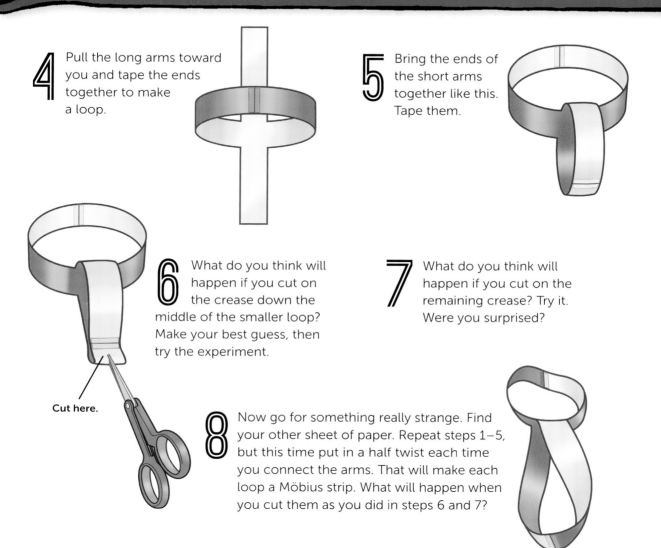

What's going on?

If all this twists your brain in a knot, that's not surprising. You've been experimenting with *topology*, a twisted area of mathematics that studies how objects change when you stretch or squeeze or tie them in knots.

According to the rules of topology, two shapes are the same if you can change one into the other by squashing or bending it. There are only two rules: you can't tear a hole in the shape or seal up any holes.

Topologists say that a donut is like a coffee cup because both have only one hole.

Table Tricks

Impossible stunts to make you the hit of any lunch table.

PAPER CLIP GRIP

What do I need?

- A $1 bill (or a long, skinny strip of paper)
- Two paper clips

What do I do?

1 Bend the dollar into an S-shape.

2 Slide the paper clips onto the S just like this.

What's going on?

If you tried the activities in Moe's Diner (pages 14–19), you may recognize this trick as a mind-twisting experiment in topology — the branch of mathematics that says a donut is like a coffee cup because both have a single hole.

The linking clips wouldn't surprise a student of topology. It's not possible to link two donuts without breaking the circle, but a paper clip isn't like a donut. It looks like a loop, but the ends of the wire aren't joined together. Since a paper clip is really just a single piece of bent wire, it's easy to join two clips by sliding the end of one wire into the loop of the other clip. In this trick, the dollar bill does that for you.

3 Hold the ends of the bill and pull. The paper clips will fly off the paper, joined together.

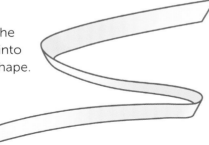

DOLLAR GRAB

What do I need?

- A bottle
- A crisp $1 bill (or a long, skinny strip of paper)
- A few coins larger than the bottle opening
- A table

Bring your finger down right here.

Make sure the bill is flat or curved upward.

What do I do?

1. Set the bottle on the table, cap off. Put the dollar on the mouth of the bottle and hold it in place with a stack of coins, as shown. The trick works best if the bill is flat or curving up a bit — not drooping downward.

2. Challenge your friend to remove the dollar without removing the coins — using only one finger.

3. After your friend gives up, wet your finger and bring it down on the dollar right near the bottle. You have to move **FAST**.

Your wet finger sticks to the dollar and yanks it downward — but the coins stay right where they are.

If you don't succeed on your first try:

- Move your finger faster. Speed is important.
- Make sure you hit the dollar close to the bottle.

What's going on?

This trick is a demonstration of *inertia*, the tendency of objects to stay put unless you give them a push. When your wet finger yanks the dollar downward, the paper rubs against the coins and pushes on them a little. But as long as the dollar is moving fast, that's not enough of a push to overcome the coins' inertia.

BALANCE A COIN [ON A] DOLLAR

What do I need?

- A crisp $1 bill (or a long, skinny piece of paper)
- A coin (the larger the coin, the easier this trick is)
- A table
- Steady hands

What do I do?

1. Fold the dollar in half, open it like a book, and stand it on the table.

2. Set the coin on the fold. The bill will support it easily.

3. Here's where you need steady hands. Grab the upper corners of the dollar and *slowly* pull them in opposite directions until the bill is almost straight. (Even when it looks straight, there's a tiny fold. That's what supports the coin.)

BALANCE A CAN [ON A] SLANT

What do I need?

- An ordinary aluminum soft drink can
- Water
- A table

What do I do?

1. If the can is empty, add water until it's about a quarter full. If it's full, drink until there's about a quarter left.

Before you try this trick at a lunch table, practice it in the kitchen sink, where a failed experiment won't be a disaster.

Tips for Master Balancers

- The bill has to be crisp. This is a great opportunity to ask a grown-up if you can borrow a bill that's worth more than whatever you have. Bills of higher value aren't used as much and are usually crisper.

- Hold the bill at the top corners when you pull. That will keep the edge steadier.

BONUS CHALLENGES

Pick up the dollar with the coin still balanced. Steady, now!

Balance three coins. Fold the bill so it looks like a W from above, set a coin on each fold, and then pull on the ends. This takes practice.

2. Take a look at the bottom of the can. You'll see that there's a slanted, or *beveled*, section connecting the side of the can with the bottom.

3. Set the can on this beveled edge and see if it balances.

If it doesn't balance, pour a little of the liquid out (or drink a little more) and try again.

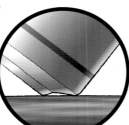

4. Once you have a feel for how much liquid you need in the can, you're ready to try it at the lunch table. Just drink until you think you have the right amount, and then check the balance. If there is still too much, drink a little more and keep testing until you get it right.

What's going on?

When you set the coin on the folded dollar, the edges of the bill hold the coin up. Those edges make an angle. As long as the center of the coin is inside that angle, the coin balances. (If you don't believe us, give it a try.)

This coin balances

This coin falls

As you straighten the dollar, the center of the coin (marked with an **x** above) always stays inside the angle made by the edges of the bill. That's because the part of the bill that has less of the coin's weight resting on it moves more than the part that has more weight on it.

The center of the coin is where its *center of gravity* is located. You can think of the center of gravity as the spot where all the coin's weight is concentrated. As long as the dollar supports the center of gravity, the coin stays balanced.

The center of gravity of the soft drink can moves around. When you tip the can, the liquid inside moves, changing the center of gravity. If the right amount of liquid is in the can, tipping it moves the center of gravity (marked with an **x**) so it is right above the beveled section. Then the can is perfectly balanced standing at a slant.

center of gravity

iMPOSSi-PiX

WHAT IS IT?
No more boring snapshots. These are photos you'll *really* want to share.

WHAT DO I NEED?
- A camera
- Some helpful friends
- Your own amazing creativity

Bottoms Up Balancer

This kid looks like he's balancing on a stack of stuff. Actually, the kid and all the stuff are lying on a sheet on the ground. We took the photo from a second-story window. Shooting from above makes all the difference.

Is this kid an incredible climber? Not really.

the HUMAN *fly*

Want to give your friend superpowers? Just use the camera angle shown in the setup.

THE SETUP

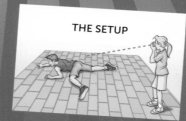

MENTAL FLOSS

Tip: Good acting will sell this illusion.

For this photo, you need three friends, a rope, and a big empty lawn or playground. Position two friends holding the rope about 15 feet (4 m) farther away than the friend whose ears will be cleaned. You can use this same setup to make an amazing video.

THE SETUP

ear cleaner #1

ear cleaner #2

photographer

Laugh Your HEAD OFF

Position your friends so the body of the head-holder hides the body of the head being held.

THE SETUP

For this photo, you need two friends and a low wall. The photographer shoots from wall-top height. The person sitting on the wall bends her neck to hide her head. And the person who is the happy head rests her chin on the wall.

THE SETUP

STARE-O-SAURUS

What is it?
A dinosaur robot that always keeps its eyes on you

What do I need?
- The Stare-O-Saurus parts
- Clear tape
- A table

How do I make it?

1 Punch out the Stare-O-Saurus pieces.

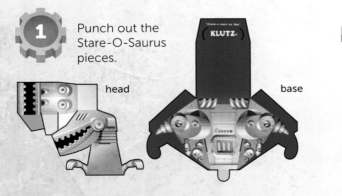

head

base

2 Lay the head on the table with the printed side up. Fold and unfold the red, blue, and gray tabs to crease them.

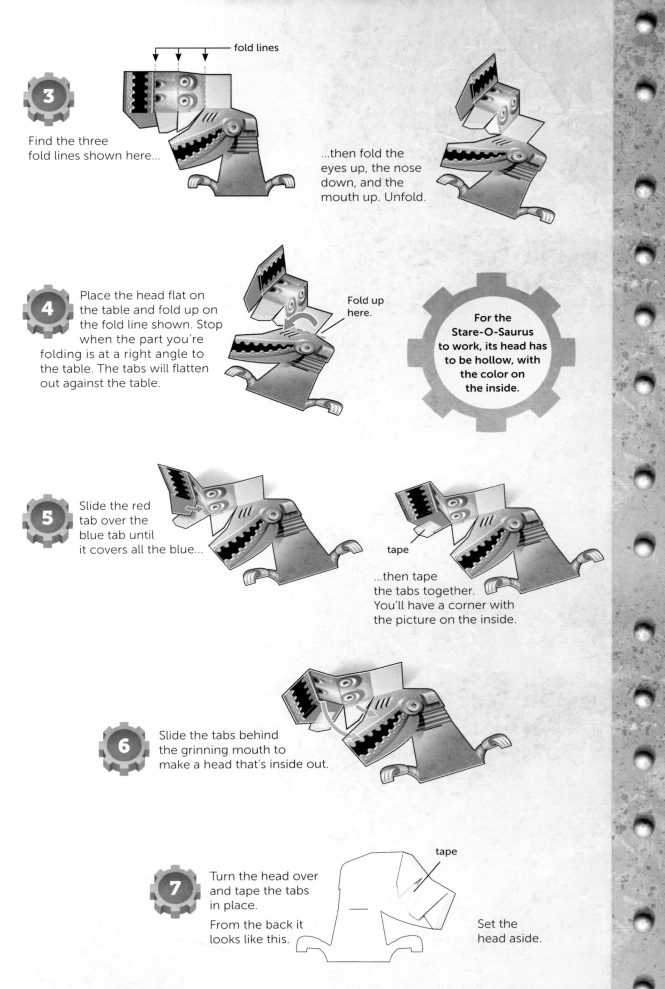

fold lines

3 Find the three fold lines shown here...

...then fold the eyes up, the nose down, and the mouth up. Unfold.

4 Place the head flat on the table and fold up on the fold line shown. Stop when the part you're folding is at a right angle to the table. The tabs will flatten out against the table.

Fold up here.

For the Stare-O-Saurus to work, its head has to be hollow, with the color on the inside.

5 Slide the red tab over the blue tab until it covers all the blue...

tape

...then tape the tabs together. You'll have a corner with the picture on the inside.

6 Slide the tabs behind the grinning mouth to make a head that's inside out.

7 Turn the head over and tape the tabs in place.

From the back it looks like this.

tape

Set the head aside.

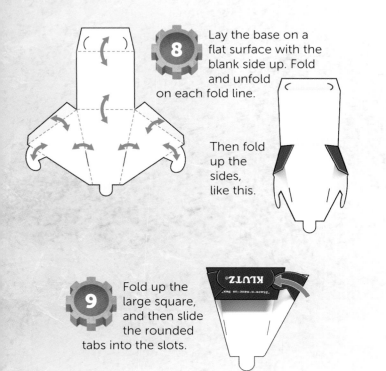

8 Lay the base on a flat surface with the blank side up. Fold and unfold on each fold line.

Then fold up the sides, like this.

9 Fold up the large square, and then slide the rounded tabs into the slots.

10 Stand the base up as shown.

On the head piece, bend the arms so they point forward. Slide them into the base and out through the slots.

tab

11 Bend the tab at the robot's neck and slide it into the slot on the head. Bend the arms out.

You're done.

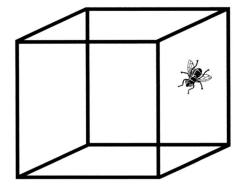

TURN THIS BOX INSIDE OUT

To play with the Stare-O-Saurus, you need to get used to turning things inside out with your mind.

Here's a clear glass box with a fly on one side. Is the fly inside the box — on the side farthest from you? Or is it outside the box — on the side closest to you?

You can see it either way, switching back and forth between the two boxes.

Once you have that down, you're ready for the Stare-O-Saurus.

What do I do with it?

1 Set your Stare-O-Saurus on a shelf. Stand about 6 feet (2 m) away and close one eye.

2 Try to see the head as a solid shape with the eyes on the outside. (That's how most people see it when they close one eye.) If you have trouble, practice with the clear glass box above, and then try again.

3 When the head looks solid, move to your right, watching the Stare-O-Saurus. The head will turn to keep an eye on you.

What's going on?

Your brain works really hard to make sense of what you see. When there are two ways to see the same thing, your brain often picks one and sticks with it. That's what's happening here.

You convinced your brain to see the Stare-O-Saurus as solid, not hollow. Then you moved — and your view of the solid head changed in a way that made sense only if the dinosaur was turning its head to follow you. Your brain took a mental shortcut — and decided that must be happening.

This is an optical illusion, a tricky situation designed to fool your eyes and brain. Closing one eye makes it easier to see the illusion because it takes away clues that would tell your brain that the head is actually hollow.

WATCH DOG

What is it?
A security guard that never goes off duty.

What do I need?
• The box that came with this book
• The watchdog cover
• Tape

What do I do?

1 Place the watchdog cover on top of the box so the eyes show through the holes. Tape the cover in place.

2 Put the watchdog in a conspicuous spot and tell your snoopy siblings you've got a new security system to watch over your stuff.

Whenever anyone walks past, they'll see the eyes following them. Researchers think that seeing images of watching eyes makes people behave better.

If you'd rather have a sentry that looks like a gigantic stone head from Easter Island, flip the watchdog cover over.

SPIN ZONE

What is it?

Eye-popping tops that change your view of the world

What do I need?

- A coin about the size of this circle (a U.S. quarter works well)
- The three spinner circles (1 thick, 2 thin)
- A smooth surface

How do I make it?

1 Slide the coin halfway through the slot in the thick spinner circle.

2 Hold on to the coin and give the top a spin. You get the best spin by holding the coin by the edge and flicking your fingers toward each other as if you were snapping them.

Time for a change?

To put a different pattern on your top, just slide a new spinner circle over the coin.

Don't miss the flip side.

There's a pattern on the front and the back of each spinner circle.

TRI-ZONAL SPACE WARPER

What do I do with it?

1 With the black and white spiral pattern facing up, spin the top fast.

2 While it's spinning, stare at the center and count slowly to 20. Then look at your hand.

3 After you recover, spin, stare, and count one more time. Then look at the picture of the snakes.

Ewww!

If your hand looked perfectly ordinary, try the experiment again, spinning the top in a brightly lit place.

What's going on?

Scientists call what you just experienced an aftereffect because looking at one thing changes what you see afterward.

Your skin isn't really crawling and those snakes aren't squirming — but they look like they are. When you stare at something in motion, your eyes and brain get tired of seeing movement in that direction. Switch to looking at something motionless, and it will look like it's moving in the opposite direction.

Jerry Andrus, a magician who was very interested in impossible objects, created and named the Tri-Zonal Space Warper. So if the snakes creeped you out, blame him.

This is not BLACK

What do I do with it?

1 Place the "THIS IS NOT BLACK" spinner circle on your top. Take a close look at the pattern. No matter what the words say, it's black and white. Or is it?

2 Give your top a spin and look again. Is it still black and white?

3 Most people see colored rings in this spinning top — even though the pattern is black and white. If you didn't see color, spin the top under a brighter light. Or try changing the speed.

4 Spin the top in the opposite direction. Is your head spinning yet?

What's going on?

Most of the time, the color you see comes from light that bounces into your eyes and makes light detectors called *cones* send signals to your brain. Red light bounces off a ripe red apple into your eyes, and the red-detecting cones tell your brain, "Hey, there's some red over there."

Cones come in three flavors. Forget strawberry, chocolate, and vanilla — these cones are red-light detectors, blue-light detectors, and green-light detectors. Every other color is made when your eyes and brain combine the signals from these three kinds of cones.

Most colors you see start with colored light, but there's no colored light bouncing off this top into your eyes. The spinning black-and-white pattern fools your eyes' cones by switching between white light (reflecting from the white part) and no light (from the black parts). White light is made of all the colors of the rainbow — so it makes all three kinds of cones signal your brain. When the black part comes along, some of the cones don't stop firing right away. The signal from these cones makes your brain think there's colored light when there really isn't.

COLORS Come and Go

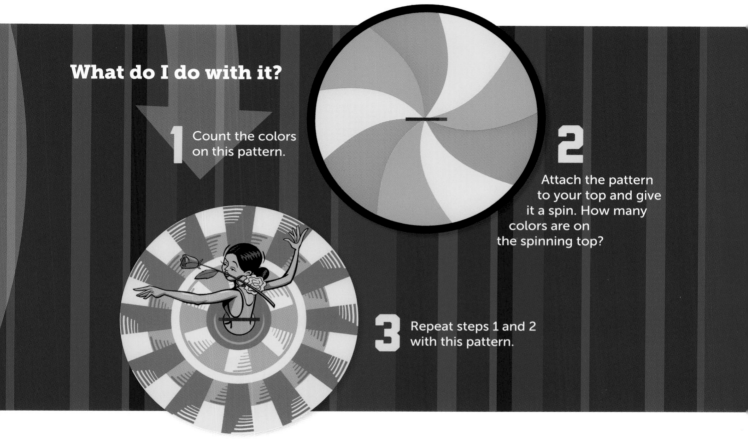

What do I do with it?

1 Count the colors on this pattern.

2 Attach the pattern to your top and give it a spin. How many colors are on the spinning top?

3 Repeat steps 1 and 2 with this pattern.

What's going on?

For almost 200 years, scientists have used tops and patterns like these in their efforts to figure out what color is and how you see it. One of the strangest things they've discovered is that color is all inside your head. Your eyes and brain are always working together to create a picture of the world — and color is part of the picture. You don't really see the world. You see the picture in your head.

The colors printed on these patterns don't change when you spin the top. But what you see does. In your eyes and brain, the colors blur together and mix. That mixing can turn bright colors into gray or white and can combine other colors to make new ones.

Make Your Own Color Spinners

Experiment with your own colored patterns. Trace the thick spinner circle on white paper, and then make a pattern on it using markers or crayons.

Check the back of the spinner circle with the dancer for a pattern created at Klutz Labs. We were inspired by the work of Marcel DuChamp, a famous artist who made spinning pictures back in the 1930s.

BALANCING ACT

An amazing acrobatic troupe with a great sense of balance

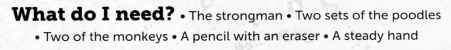

STRONGMAN
AND HIS
ANIMALS

What do I need? • The strongman • Two sets of the poodles
• Two of the monkeys • A pencil with an eraser • A steady hand

What do I do?

1 Fold the strongman and the poodles on the center crease, and then flatten them. When you're done, each piece will have a slight bend down the middle.

2 Hold the pencil with the eraser pointed up. Set the tip of the strongman's chin on the eraser. He will balance with his feet stretched out almost level.

Remove the strongman, and balance a set of the poodles, setting the middle poodle's nose on the eraser.

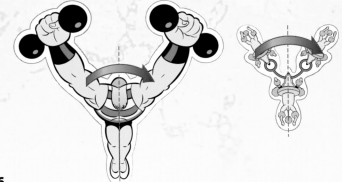

BALANCE CHALLENGES

Hold the pencil sideways. Balance a set of poodles on one end and the strongman on the other. The pencil's point makes balancing harder, but you can do it.

Hook a monkey's arm over the pencil and balance the strongman on the monkey's tail.

Hook a monkey on each of the strongman's arms and balance him on the pencil's eraser. Adding monkeys makes the strongman tip forward, but he stays balanced.

What's going on?

You can make just about anything balance if you put a support under just the right spot. That spot is called the *balance point*. For the strongman, the balance point is right at the tip of his chin.

Once the strongman is balanced, you can gently tap his feet or push them to one side — the strongman will rock and spin and still stay balanced.

That's because his center of gravity is in just the right place. You can think of the center of gravity as the spot where all the weight of an object is concentrated. When the strongman is folded slightly on his center line, his center of gravity is a little less than half an inch (1.3 cm) below his chin.

Having the center of gravity below the balance point makes the strongman a great balancer. Pushing his feet down lifts his center of gravity up. Gravity, the force that pulls you toward the center of the Earth, pulls his center of gravity back down, returning the strong man to a perfectly balanced position.

balance point

center of gravity

★ ALL STAR ★
ACROBATS

Put together a top-notch circus act

What do I need?
• The strongman • The monkeys • The poodles
• The bear • The acrobat and elephant
• Two chairs and a ruler or a broom arranged as shown.

(If your balancer slips on the broom, wrap a piece of masking tape around the handle and balance your acrobat there.)

balance point

balance point

ACROBAT & ELEPHANT

BALANCING BEAR

What do I do?

1. Set the edge of the acrobat's umbrella on the broom or ruler. Slowly loosen your hold and let her find her balance.

2. Hold the elephant steady and balance a set of the poodles on his foot. Then let go.

1. Set the bear's wheel on the broom or ruler and let him balance.

2. Hold the bear steady and hang a monkey from each barbell. Let go and he'll still balance.

What's going on?

You can balance an entire acrobatic troupe on the acrobat and elephant. That's because the center of gravity, the spot where the weight is concentrated, is far below the balance point. (See page 37 for more on this.) The bear's low-hanging barbells keep him stable by lowering his center of gravity.

CAN YOU TOP THIS?

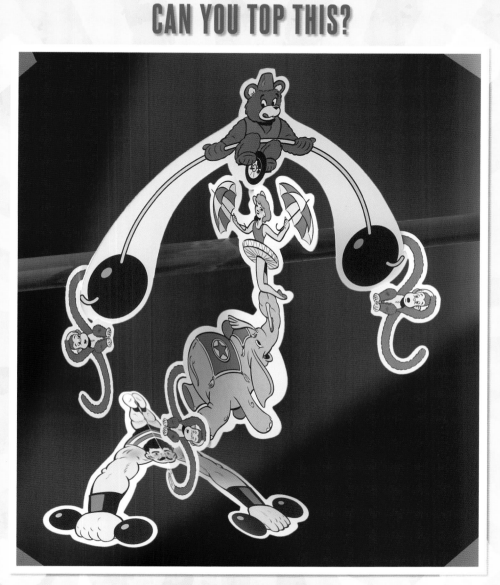

Use your acrobats to make a really spectacular balancing act.
Here are some combinations to try.

★ Start with the acrobat and elephant. Balance the bear on the elephant's back, and then add the strongman to the acrobat's foot.

★ Add a set of poodles to each of the acrobat's umbrellas.

★ Hook a monkey to each of the bear's barbells, and then balance a set of poodles on each monkey's tail.

If you have trouble, have a friend hold one piece steady while you balance another piece on it.

THE LABYRINTH

WELCOME TO THE LABYRINTH WONDERS AWAIT YOU... JUST DON' GET LOST

What is it?

A folded piece of paper — from which you may never escape

What do I need?

The labyrinth • A table • Clear tape

How do I make it?

1. Carefully punch out the square piece in the middle.

2. Find the corner with the yellow circle. Lay the paper on the table with **1** in the lower left corner. Fold so **1** lands on **2**.

3. Find the blue square in the upper left corner. Fold **3** so it lands on **4**.

4. Find the purple triangle in the upper right corner. Fold **5** so it lands on **6**.

5. Find the green diamonds. Fold **7** so it lands on **8**.

6. Fold the blue stars so [9] lands on [10].

7. Fold the green clovers so [11] lands on [12].

8. Being careful not to let any folds come unfolded, flip the whole paper over.

9. Fold the purple moons so [13] lands on [14]. Hold this flap down while you do the next step.

10. Fold the orange hearts so [15] lands on [16]. Almost there!

11. Pick up the top two layers of the lower left square. Fold these layers so [17] lands on [18].

End up like this:

12. On the square with the purple moon [13], there's a blue outline. Pick up your labyrinth. See how the outline continues on the other side? Stick a piece of tape across the blue outline so it holds the sides together. Make sure it is secure.

That's it! Your labyrinth is finished. Turn the page to see how to navigate this maze and find the treasure.

What do I do with it?

Fold and unfold the labyrinth to find the treasure hidden deep within the paper.

Here's how to start your search.

1 Flip the labyrinth to the side with the "Welcome" message.

2 Close the labyrinth like you're shutting a book, folding the outer edges together toward you.

3 Now, open it the same way, but from the *back side*. You'll see a new picture — the first stop on your trip through the labyrinth.

4 Now you have a choice of how to proceed. You can try:
- closing and opening the labyrinth a second time, just as you did in steps 2–3
- rotating the labyrinth a quarter turn and then repeating steps 2–3
- flipping the whole labyrinth over

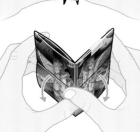

At any point, you have these three choices (although they might not all work).

Your goal is to find the treasure and then reach the stairs to the surface. **GOOD LUCK!**

IF YOU GET STUCK

There are two dead ends. If it seems like you can't go further, try flipping the labyrinth over and folding from there.

You'll often see pieces of a different room around the edges of the one you're currently in. Chances are, the complete picture of that room is just a fold and a flip away.

There are ten rooms in the labyrinth. How many did you find?

- **Entrance Cavern**
- **Dark Well**
- **Column Hallway**
- **Slimy Tunnel**
- **Candlelit Temple**
- **Minotaur**
- **The Hooded One**
- **Spider Queen**
- **Treasure**
- **Stairway to the Surface**

Once you've escaped with the treasure, challenge friends and grown-ups to navigate the maze.

BEWARE THE DANGERS OF THE LABYRINTH!

On your way down, the rope started to fray
To make it back out, you must find a new way

Each tunnel and chasm could spring a foul trap
(If only the rats hadn't eaten your map!)

One candle burns bright at the stone temple door
For every poor soul that was lost here before

The Minotaur's prowling to pulverize thieves
"That treasure is mine!" (Or so he believes)

There it is! Shining jewels and mountains of dough
Better fill up your pockets, still halfway to go

The Hooded One spells certain doom for your quest:
That candle's for you — are you lost like the rest?

The exit awaits at the top of the stair,
But first you must pass through the Spider Queen's lair

You've made it! You've faced all the perils and won!
Unless Minotaur's gold disappears in the sun...

What's going on?

This weird object is called a *flexagon*. Most folded pieces of paper change size when you unfold them. With this flexagon, you can do the same fold twice in a row and the paper will stay the same size: fold once and the center becomes the edges, fold again and the edges return to the center.

Flexagons were invented in 1939 by a Princeton student named Arthur H. Stone. Because his English-size paper didn't fit into American-size notebooks, he trimmed off the edges and then started playing around with the leftover strips. One of Stone's classmates, Richard Feynman, helped him come up with different kinds of flexagons. Feynman later became one of the most important scientists of the 20th century. It just goes to show that sometimes the best inspiration comes when you should be doing your homework.

ACETATE ANIMATIONS

What is it?

Mini-movies made from sliced-up pictures

What do I need?

• The animations slider

What do I do?

1 Set the slider on top of the dragon below, lining up the clear arrows on the slider with the black arrows on the page.

2 Slowly move the slider from side to side.

What's going on?

Lift off the slider and look closely at the dragon's flames. You'll see three sets of stripes that don't quite line up with each other. Each set makes a different part of the flames.

The slider's black bars are wide enough to cover two sets of stripes. When the slider is lined up, you see only one set of stripes, which makes one

part of the flames. As you move the slider, you uncover different stripes, making the flames flicker as some parts appear and others disappear. Your eyes and brain put the different pictures together so you see a single picture that looks like it's moving.

Use the slider with the other pictures to make them move.

RATOSCOPE

What is it?

A circle of scurrying rats.
(You say they aren't scurrying?
Just wait.)

What do I need?

The Ratoscope • A pencil with an eraser
A pushpin • A mirror

What do I do?

1 Punch out the Ratoscope.

2 Stick the pushpin through the middle of the rat side of the Ratoscope and into the eraser of the pencil.

← This is the side with rats on it.

3 Stand in front of a mirror, spin the Ratoscope, and look through the little slits at the reflection. The rats will start scurrying. (We told you so.)

What's going on?

When you spin the wheel and look at the mirror through the slits, you see the rats as a series of still pictures with gaps between them. In each picture, the rats are in a slightly different position. When the wheel spins fast enough and the gaps are small enough, your eyes and brain blend the still pictures, filling in the gaps to make a single moving picture.

This kind of moving picture toy was invented about 150 years ago. Back then, people called it a phenakistoscope. Since that's tough to say, we are calling this one a Ratoscope.

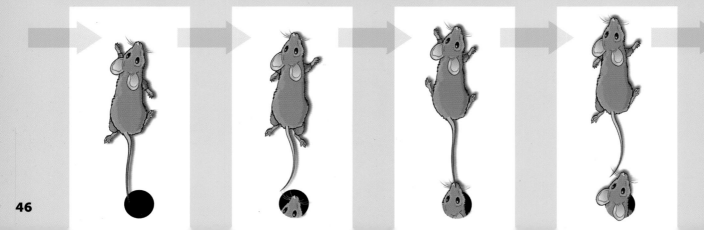